S0-EGG-876

life is not what

we think it

is,

it's only what we

imagine it to

be

Charles Bukowski

FRAGMENTS

FRAGMENTS

A Book of
Poetry

Emmett Wheatfall

FRAGMENTS
©2015 by Emmett Wheatfall

All rights reserved. No part of this publication may be repro-
duced, stored in a retrieval system or transmitted in any form or
by any means, electronic, mechanical, photocopying, recording,
scanning or otherwise, except as permitted under code 107 or
108 of the 1976 United States Copyright Act, without prior writ-
ten permission of the author. Requests for permission should
be addressed to:

ewheatfall@gmail.com
P.O. Box 30105
Portland, OR 97294

Cover Design by—Clark Graphics
Poetry Editor—Eric Alder

ISBN 978-0-9965296-0-0
Library of Congress Control Number 2015945287
First Printing, September 2015

Printed in the United States of America

Reflections Publishing House
http://reflectph.com

To my wife,
Karen Wheatfall

You never get the meaning of any of my poems.
However, you've listened patiently to
every one of them.

Thank You.

Contents

FOREWORD

We Imagine Ourselves as a Whole,
But Remember Ourselves as Fragments

The word *fragment* literally means something broken or
cut off, something detached from the whole, an imper-
fection. Such fragmentary lyrics and poems are exem-
plified in the works of modernist poets like Ezra
Pound's *The Cantos* (1915–1969), Louis Zukofsky's
 "A" (1927–1978), and T.S. Eliot's "The Waste Land"
(1922) (Hirsch.) Historically, fragmented works or texts
were expected as a result of a past not entirely intact.
As W. R. Johnson puts it in *The Idea of Lyric*
 (1982.)

No experience in reading, perhaps, is more depressing
and more frustrating than to open a volume of Sap-
pho's fragments and to recognize, yet again—one al-
ways hopes that somehow this time it will be different—
that this poetry is all but lost to us. . . . Even though we
know that Greek lyric is mere fragments, in-
deed, *because* we know that Greek lyric is mere frag-
ments, we act, speak, and write as if the unthinkable

had not happened, as if pious bishops, careless monks, and hungry mice had not consigned Sappho and her lyrical colleagues to irremediable oblivion. (Johnson qtd in Hirsch.)

These fragmented texts are the ruins of obsession. Readers spent lifetimes searching for finished writings rotted out from the seams of books as well as fragments of writings and drawings from the prehistoric to the medieval to the Renaissance eras. Anne Janowitz suggest the romantic fragment is "a *partial whole*— either a remnant of something once complete and now broken or decayed, or the beginning of something that remains unaccomplished" (Janowitzqtd in Hirsch.) The fragment becomes a period in time that can never be put back together, never completed or put in order. Perhaps this is the infinite beauty of the fragment— incompleteness, an interruption in time that breaks off from a universal system.

Even literatures of trauma and writing to heal are strewn with a fragmented language, which evolved out of the stimulus of psychosomatic pain. This includes

Aristotle's notions of catharsis and Arthur W. Frank's *The Wounded Storyteller*, which explores the relation to bodies and narratives. Consider Virginia Woolf's trauma-laden *Mrs. Dalloway*, a text dominated by the shell-shocked ex-soldier Septimus Warren Smith; and by the whisper and momentary reference to the death of Sylvia Parry, Clarissa Dalloway's sister. *To the Lighthouse* was an elegy to Woolf's deceased parents, and *The Waves* is read in flashbacks and disorientation of the psyche. Woolf's suffering provided her with creative stimulation through semi-spiritual visualizations of transcendence. Her writing was intuitive of an otherwise un-resolved life of psychological affliction.

It is words that acknowledge life's void, its gaping holes and periods of silence, breaks from the world. Freud even confessed, in *Civilization and its Discontents,* that it was the philosopher-poet Schiller that revealed to him that the mechanism of the world was held together by "hunger and love." From Schiller, **Freud recognized two basic instincts: sex and the self-preservation** instinct. He admired the poet's ability to have access to psychological truths, and wrote of

Goethe in particular: "One may well sigh when one realizes that it is nevertheless given to a few to draw the most profound insights, without any real effort, from the maelstrom of their own feelings, while we others have to grope our way restlessly to such insights through agonizing insecurity" (Goethe qtd in Freud). Perhaps what Freud uncovered is that writing maintains our conviction in meaning, our belief, in Yeats' odd phrase that "words alone are certain good," and that words can connect or disconnect us from the whole (Yeats.)

In his new collection, *Fragments*, Emmett Wheatfall does just this: introduce us to the breaks in time, the interruptions of thoughts and feelings that seem to come almost randomly. He suggests that to find the language of life, one must come to represent metaphorical and literal breaks in memory, rather than the grammar and terminologies of ordinary life experiences. There must be a more accurate language to describe the un-whole, the gaps, the parts where one "cannot hear/ not because he wants to /but because he can."

His fragmentary writing investigates what Jean-Francois Lyotard, the French philosopher and literary theorist known for his articulation of postmodernism after the late 1970s— calls the different, or the *feeling* one cannot find the words. He notes that what is at stake in literature is to bear witness by finding a language for this unrepresentable feeling, for these fragmented, out of place moments in life. Wheatfall ventures into the silence, "and when that becomes nothing," he "masters something new." Each poem suggests that with each break, with each slice into reality, that there is actually something whole being constructed, created. This fragmented language proves that "life stand[s] still" not because we are in awe of its majestic moments, but because we become conscious of our broken time, of our small part in the whole. The poems in *Fragments* remind us that each part of our lives is an emancipation where we "[feast] on every memory of [this] short-lived" life.

Such fragmentary writing reminds me of a small anecdote about the Argentine writer Jorge Luis Borges regarding the representation of truth in narrative. While on a trip to the Sahara, Borges cupped some sand in his palm and dropped it in another location. He later wrote in his journal: "I am modifying the Sahara" (Borges qtd in Ruefle 3.) This turned out to be one of the most prominent memories of his trip. The point is we aren't saving the Sahara, we aren't saving anything— we are adjusting it. Understanding the fragmentary nature of life and writing is about personal rendering, the possibility of arranging the "out-of-order signs," as Mary Ruefle puts it. Writing about life's fragments suggests a reality that offers a "humanness in which we are able to imagine ourselves" again (Strand qtd in Boland xxi.)

Loren Kleinman

The Dark Cave between My Ribs & Breakable Things

Sources

Boland, Eavan. "Poetic Form: A Personal Encounter by Eavan Boland." *The Making of a Poem*. London: W.W. Norton and Company, 2000. Conrad, Joseph. *Heart of Darkness: An Authoritative Text, Backgrounds and Sources, Criticism*. Ed. Robert Kimbrough. New York: Norton, 1971. PrintDerrida, Jacques. Force and Signification, in *Writing and Difference*. London: Routledge, 1978. Trans. Alan Bass. (pp 1-36). Print.

Frank, Arthur W. *The Wounded Storyteller.* Chicago: University. of Chicago Press, 1995. Print. Freud, Sigmund. *Penguin Freud Library.* "Creative Writers and Day-Dreaming," in PFL 14, *Art and Literature.* London: Penguin, 1990. (pp 131-141). Print. Hirsch, Edward. "From A Poet's Glossary: Fragment." Poets.org. 2014.Web. 6 May 2015. Ruefle, Mary. "Sincere Irreverence," in *American Poet: The Journal of American Poets.* Vol. 26, Spring 2004. (pp 4-6) Woolf, Virginia. *Mrs. Dalloway.* Oxford: Oxford University Press, 2000. Print Yeats, William Butler. *Words Alone Are Certain Good William Butler Yeats: Himself. The Poet. His Ghost.*The Dolmen Press, Dublin; First Edition, 1961. Print.

Antiquity

Caveman's Wall

I say open the tombs and tomes where
knowledge is hid, held hostage and imprisoned.
Decipher the hieroglyphics inscribed upon
the caveman's wall; the writings of Egyptians, the
noted works of Essenes; lest we forget
what we've known, what we've lost, who we are,
and what we might become.

Graffiti

its patterns,
every stroke, decoupled from
intent and cognitive imagination
comes from somewhere,
as desire dictated by
impulse

without borders.
the lines flow like wild rivers
unabridged by
banks with ambiguous lines
only paper reveals

Someone Has Written Something

Its letters of alphabet
do not form words. Of what is left
I discern very little. Someone has
written something. Nothing
makes sense.

Madness knows too much. Too
much! Far from a cry is a single
teardrop. In madness a smile trumps
a frown. For this my world has
gone mad.

Open Walls

I see more clearly now
Scratching long verse
On these open walls
Between these iron bars
With my dissident mind

Lore

Legends and Myths

These questions are not of legend,
nor of myth; these are matters
of truth. Fools despise truth. And who
among us has never been a fool?

Dragons

Death haunts me daily.
It is not an aberration,
nor my inclination.
The dragons are real;
the skin grafts are mine.

Antithesis

Deceit is the antithesis of honesty.

Such enlightenment
is well known
by presbyters and pontiffs,
delighting mythological gods like
Prometheus,
who stole celestial fire
and brought it to earth.

Enlightenment

Collective Essence

The collective essence of all things originated
from something.

Is that something God?
I don't know.

However, I do suggest this thought came from

something.

Monk of Ennui

He cannot not hear; not because he wants to,
but because he can. Even though hymns play
loudly, he chooses to visit paradise, to venture
into the silence of sequestration, to that conclave
within himself as the Monk of Ennui

Coming Was the Revelation

Can a flame give life to fire without a spark?
Can a spark give life to a flame without kindling?
Coming was the revelation;
And she was in labor.

How does the seer see being blind?
What does the prophet know without being told?
Coming was the revelation;
And she was in labor.

Something Holy

Assemble a Pentecostal choir.

The Seraphim have already convened.

This is not a matter of the heart.

Think wind, think spirit, and sing the doxology.

The two of you could have been friends.

Who knows, you might see each other again.

Inhale its breath; take into you its life.

Recall that it had a name. Even a pronoun has

significance. I know this speak of madness.

I know this speaks of madness.

One Borrowed Tomb

You, clay Zeus.
You, mounted mute—
etched in stone:

there is but one borrowed tomb.

It's empty.

The Last Death

I recall my firstborn's birth

Afterward I stood still

Who will recall the last death

And will that life stand still

Edification

The Cycle

in the winter

there is darkness

from spring comes birth

summer the season of life

the fall—death

this is the cycle

in the winter

...

No Destiny

The sea never fails me before the setting sun.
I see manatees swimming swiftly below me,
sea turtles swimming away on the surface
of soundless waves like sea-urchins with no   des-
tiny,
sharks stalking simple-minded fish conjured up
in my sense of savagery. I savor the moment.

Windbreaker

Like a schooner, having not
set itself to sail, I feel the nudge.
As if mute, I want to speak:
I sense inspiration.

Bug

In and of themselves, the world above ground,
and the one underground are dangerous.
When the two intersect I'm made to feel
like an insect.

Mindfulness

We Were Special

We were mere raindrops on the landscape of life,

whereupon,

in the morning,

we returned from where we came,

for we were refreshed,

we were special.

Strike A Pose

When the stars appear
in their fixed positions, I will count them one by one,
bundling them in dozens;

then strike a pose to mark the moment.

Minions

I sit among the plumb apple trees

Pleasured by their fruit-bearing seed

Relieved of minions from failures past

I, for now, sit unmasked

Gopher Holes

In the landscape
there are gopher holes.

Once you've seen the light,
then you will know the depth and breadth
of my darkness.

Ambient Noise

As I enter the latter part of my life
I'm learning to silence its ambient noise,
focusing only on the angelic humming
of iridescent hummingbirds.

Madness

A clown
posited out of context
is certainly something made
of madness.

Self-determination

Some Were Fools

I've seen the mighty fall,
the fearful consumed.

Some were fools. The wise,
their knowledge,
they failed to pass on.

Know Yourself

The beauty of *you* in America is that
you can be whoever *you* perceive yourself to be.
It's always best when *you* know yourself—
for yourself.

Equilibrium

Through my blindness I travel
With all but my whistle and gavel
Faith & hope my scepter my mantle
Through my blindness I travel

Equilibrium no longer my plum line
A sensory experience for my kind
A bushel of worth for the sublime
Equilibrium no longer my plum line

Gullible

how pompous
the panhandler can be
opining lies wherewith
to make his plea

plying alongside
this, a busy street:
insensitive a bastard he
makes of me

deceiving me, the gullible
predicate I be

Unrepressed Affluence

Bubbling up is the beauty of a surrendered   dis-
position,
repositioning itself with unrepressed affluence,
reaching for the light of life from the depths of the
dark deep.

Consequence

To act without knowledge of consequence
is to be without conscience.

Majestic

Master something—
and when that becomes nothing,
master something new. For therein
lies the majestic.

Hamlet's Advice

Fool!
Do not saw the air, sir
...
Be angry
But sin not

Caesar

If a blossom, you being stiff-necked
would be understandable,
given your gold crown and leafy petals.

But we know,

You will never be a Caesar

This Man

Unable to walk,
he recalls the roads less traveled,
and longs again for their

anticipation.

Unable to taste, he
feasts on every memory
of his short-lived

emancipation.

Nationalism

We the People

A nation will never know its true economic viability, when lost is the redemptive capacity of poor people, people of color, the uneducated and marginalized citizen.

Never forget: It's "*WE* the people," America.

Patriotism

I know why mankind never went back to the moon

Even why he left that place so littered with junk

A space mobile that's no longer salvageable

Packets of orange-flavored Tang and the U.S. flag

Which use to satisfy his big thirst for patriotism

American Way

Is the answer to police brutality and militarism the Second Amendment to the United States Constitution?

That's the American way isn't it?

Black Friday

Bread-lines are forming everywhere
Every day is *Black Friday* for many
Milk cans now hold change not milk
Replace the box-spring mattress
Whose only yield is a night's sleep
The milk can investment—nil
Guess who milks cows now

Ethnicity

Definition

He is more than the definition assigned his skin color,
the marginalized veracity of his intellect, and the
misguided stereotypical assumption about his t emperament
(angry black man.)

No. He is a pastor, poet, public sector professional;
a faithful husband, father, and good citizen.

Stop getting it twisted, okay?

Mustard Tannin

The dark side of my skin amazes me.

Its mustard tannin mixed with charcoal
colored Crayola.

I'm stained for life. A stick figure weighed
down by fat.

They say I'm a big man.

The foghorn in the harbor is my voice,
bellowing across the bow of my

influence, singularly warning harbor-mooring
fools it's me.

Negro Napoleon

I am not the first of my kind,
made of flesh and blood, to suck
from black breasts, nibble on
my mother's fingertips.

I thought myself a Caesar once,
maybe the first Negro Napoleon.
My *no's* ruled the world then.

Southern Style

Facing dirt-dusty roads

These men rock their rocking chairs

On rickety a riddled porch

The rhythm—that of a strong man

Making love to a fine-ass woman

With what cannot be mentioned

Nor written

It being just about all any women

Or rickety porch

Can handle

Brother

The white man down South,

he calls us, well, *colored*.

But his son,

he wants to be a brother.

Negro Poets

Hot from a day's pickin'
We witness the diminution
Of our *poesies*

Live long Negro voices
Imprinted on white pages
Of self-published press

We Negro poets
We sing not of America
We write the Negro witness

New Black

Orange is the new black
Jumpsuit plus-size and brown eyes
Me—a woman, her man

Inequity

Racism

Someone asked, "If racism is a disease,
then how can it be cured? Any ideas? Thoughts?"
I replied, "There is no cure.
Stop looking for it."

Stonewall

Stonewall Jackson
is glazed brown now.
So reminiscent is he of the slave,
who to a slave,
labored under blazing sun.
He knows stone-walls have come down.
Civil war is over,
civil rights breathe life.

Urban Pioneers

Ubiquitous the change.
Blatant the disregard for history, the
heritage preceding these young,

white, urban pioneers. As if
the West needs settlers—

settling again.

Infamy

In a sea of obscurity,

black men live in infamy,

while whitey commemorates historically,

one small step for man,

one small step for mankind.

Sweet-Bird Sing

Was it when that gay boy
said, *"Hey!"*
Or was it when Little Big-Mama said,
"Baby brown boy, you so pretty!"
Or was it when the soapbox preacher
stopped preaching hate?

Listen.

Vantage Points

Blackbirds refuse to eat stale white bread

As the rest of the world watches from vantage points

Of mountains and below sea level

Mockingbirds

...still,

they deny me the beauty of a bird's flight.
Eagerly from the same stream we drink. Bitter
does the trickling water taste.

It is not for you
that this poem is written,
but for me,
and mothers of mockingbirds.

Interrelational

Hearts

"Draw something" she said. And I
stroked twelve concentric hearts
before her eyes.

And she loved me for it.

Burning Essence

Succulent these tender teasing
Stolen in several seconds of kissing
Where *no* never means *no*

And, yes

The burning essence of

...

Are We One

"Are we one?"

Chances are you didn't know until now. A
squawking crow distracts as mists of rain fall.
Trust this voice and imagine smelling fresh air,
feel seasonal spring chill. Acquainted now? My
words, your voice—conflation?

"Are we one?"

Star-Crossed

If beached whales like seafaring mariners
on occasion lose their way; what then is to be said about
star-crossed lovers?

Empty Reminder

A faceless picture
is in frame
as empty reminder
of what was, and will
never again be.

Silly Hearts

We two are fools dislodged by silly hearts
No matter her affection won at night

Let the truth judge between me and thee, sir
A deceived heart is worse when left to err

So put down your fists for trifling affect
Gather yourself before your face I wreck

A woman's love is never worth the fight
No matter her affection won at night

Feline Fluency

This is her garden

the wailing wall of her vitriol,

a sanctum for her polemic,

wherein no arbiter

tends,

where unprecedented reason

finds safe harbor

in feline fluency.

Blossom Blue

Wistful love from once
a backward blossom; blue,
now reddish plum.

Thirst

You are distilled—yet water.

And I thirst for what remains.

Unbeknown to Men

The most dangerous woman, unbeknown to men,
is the one who genuinely listens.

Forget Me Not

My friend abandoned our friendship.

I was aboard when he set fire to our ship.

Him being far ashore; and me—left to burn

as our mask and hull still burn.

I'm covered in friendship's ashes and soot.

He's saved himself—but left me burning

on the sea of belief—far from reality's relief.

No greater love hath any man than this,

that lay down his life for his friend.

He's now living on shores called—*Moved On,*

while I'm drowning in a vast ocean of

a million moments called *Forget Me Not.*

My friend abandoned our friendship.

Manning the Oars

I will not return to the mountains behind me;
they being the backbone of Crete. No, I will
always stand ashore, manning the oars of my soul
until the tide never recedes again, as do we
weary men, who long for love.

Salina, Kansas

Someone before me has etched
the initials E.W. into the window. Ironically,
those are my initials. I need to put
my pocket knife away. It has a tendency
to get me in trouble.

My overhead light isn't working. It's
half-past midnight. I'm half-asleep. I'm
half-way home. Salina, Kansas
waits for me.

Epiphany

Marvin

Just because you write prose,

doesn't mean you can write prosody.

Poetry is not strawberry sweet cream,

found in some soda fountain shop

where Marvin Gaye belts out

a tune from the belly of a jukebox.

Samuel Jackson

I linger too long between sentiments
Mutha-fucker, may I
Mutha-fucker, I may not
Certainly transitive: overtly sensitive

Jah, bless Samuel Jackson

Linda Hornbuckle

It's all good. She be happy now.

Lovely as a lark Linda was. A singing lark Linda was.
Soulful, sultry, and sensuous as she could be—
angelic in grace and faith too.

...

It's all good. She be happy now.

Dylan Thomas

Read aloud the verse of Dylan Thomas
    At sunset salvation will come
Therefore, a drunken stupor must not arise
    Single-out wine, flat bread, and humus

Goad his metaphors and similes
    Let them glisten like un-tinted glass
Fashion an elegy befitting evening
    Think Dylan Thomas and me

Revelation

When Rain Falls

Cunning conundrum

are days

when rain fails while the sun shines

and I'm alive

Summer Sun

We need not upbraiding, we are
the sun's subjects for the sheer will of it—
nothing more, nothing less.

If only you understood humility.

What a gift of sight.

Anecdotal

Waddling Down the Road

the invisible lines
blocking the door of a
"Colored Only" bar,
or the rhythmic suggestion in a
smooth jazz melody, being spoken
without speaking;

projecting pessimism
without a purpose,
living knowing it's the dying
that's coming
when waddling down the road with a
bobble-head affixed to a backpack,
you burst with bundles of pride
for coming newborn baby;

She Doesn't Play There Now

There, people have never heard of her
because she doesn't play there now.
She's buried at the bottom of the hillside,
overlooking the river basin miles away.

Chopping Sound

It is not his time. Mornings belong to the baker,
not the butcher. Mornings are for rolling; not the
chop,
chop,
chop,
chopping sound slapping against the cutting-board.
Morning is for sweet things, not the salty taste of
things to come in the evening.

Carl bakes in the morning;

Karl in the coming evening.

Night Watchman

Closed!
The crooked window sign reads.
...
Fading is the night watchman's whistle.
At its end he will retire.

Concrete City

With its matchstick looking streetlights
Its towering beehives of busy bodies
Where fiefdoms and tribal living exist
Gentrification as if it were plankton
Streets stretching like surgical suture
Color-coded men terrorize the community
Cops that are on call 24-hours a day
Out of the wild I have come
Having left behind the concrete city

On Either Side

Opposite the door,
at the window, a violent predator waits.
Fingers gripping the window sill,
eyes parallel the bottom window frame,
a wool cap keeps his head warm,
and a little boy trembles in fright
under his bed sheets.

On either side of him is possibility.

Inspiration

Soul Sing

A song refreshes the moment,
then quickly dissipates as if a morning's dew.

Sing, my soul, sing!

Poetry Books by Emmett Wheatfall

He Sees Things

We Think We Know

The Meaning of Me

Bread Widow

AFTERWORD

Given that you are reading this Afterword, you have more than likely read *Fragments*. I want to thank a dear poetry friend of mine named Loren Kleinmann for the beautiful foreword she's written for this work. Loren is an exceptional poet in her own right and has honored me by writing what amounts to an academic affirmation of the concept of Fragments—which is not novel, as she so aptly points out. Great poets who've preceded me have taken to pen and paper with the intent to offer fragmented poems as individual poetic pieces, so her exposition is a treasure I will forever hold dear in my poetic journey.

A. J. Hayes and Anthony Desmond are two African American poets I greatly admire. Prolific writers in their own right both have offered affirming commentary on this collection. I just felt I needed some keen and discerning eyes to examine these fragments as excerpts from their source of origin. I offer a very sincere and heartfelt "thank you" to A. J. Hayes and Anthony Desmond for their assistance.

A friend of mine named Eric Alder has stepped forward and consented to be my personal poetry editor. Eric's assistance with this collection of poems has been invaluable. There is nothing more freeing for a poet than to have his or her trusted editor evaluate the work with the intent to make it the best it can possibly be. I revel in his suggestions, offered without expectation of adherence and undue influence. By way of analogy, he keeps me in my lane in the pool, always rooting me on by the inspiration he derives from each work. I look forward to us working together more so in the days and years to come. Thank you, Eric.

Fragments represent my 5th book with Reflections Publishing House. Deborah Bellis, the owner, knows how hard it is to work with writers. I would imagine I'm no different. Reflections Publishing House has been committed to me as a publisher who thinks highly of my poetics. I'm proud of the work we have put forth to the literary world and lovers of poetry. Thank you, Reflections Publishing House.

I think it's fitting I share the following anecdote: When I first considered taking the writing of poetry seriously, I asked a prominent poet and teacher of poetry if he'd mentor me. Given his stature, I was quite surprised when he said yes. After publishing my first collection of poetry, he told me that poetry book would be, in essence, the marker by which I will measure my growth as a poet. I sincerely believe *Fragments* reveals my growth as a poet.

I hope you've enjoyed this work. Don't forget, these poems are 'fragments' of previously written poems staged as standalone works. Thank you!

Emmett Wheatfall

ABOUT THE AUTHOR

Emmett Wheatfall lives in Portland, Oregon where he reads, writes, and performs poetry. He has self-published four books of poetry entitled He Sees Things (2010) We Think We Know (2011) The Meaning of Me (2012) and Bread Widow (2013).

Emmett has written four chapbooks under the titles *Queen of the Nile*, *I Too Am A Slave*, *The Majestic*, and *Midnight In Madrid*. His poems have been published in online journals and periodicals.

Mr. Wheatfall has released one non-lyrical poetry CD titled *I Speak*, and three lyrical poetry CDs. *When I Was Young* (2010) is a thematic CD that speaks to love, hope, betrayal, and fidelity addressed in various social and cultural context. *I Loved You Once* (2011) contains poetry writing set to jazz, blues, and pop music. His latest release, *Them Poetry Blues* (2013), is a compilation of great poetry contextualize in blues genre. It's an album featuring some of Oregon's most talented jazz and blues musicians.

He served on the Nomination Committee for the selection of 2014 Oregon Poet Laureate Peter Sears. The Oregon Poet Laureate fosters the art of poetry, encourages literacy and learning, addresses central issues related to humanities and heritage, and reflects on public life in Oregon. The poet is appointed by the governor of the State of Oregon.

Emmett has been a featured poet at numerous poetry readings and has performed lyrical poetry in concert with Oregon Poet Laureate, Lawson Inada, He has been on the radio with Oregon's Poet Laureate, Paulann Petersen, and has been an active participant in the Portland Poetry Slam (PPS) spoken word scene.

He was a featured poet at the 50th *Anniversary Celebration of the March on Washington,* a Portland event, where he delivered his original poem *Miles To Go Before We Sleep,* written for the occasion.

Emmett was the keynote speaker at the Oregon Historical Society's Oregon Black History Series "*March on Washington for Jobs and Freedom Fiftieth Anniversary Programs*" screening of Dr. King's famous "*I Have A Dream*" speech.

A special mention is made of his longtime personal assistant, Ms. Carolyn Lee and poetry editor, Eric Alder.

CPSIA information can be obtained at www.ICGtesting.com
Printed in the USA
LVOW03*1733040915

452518LV00004B/5/P